WILDLIFE FUN

Would you like to draw your favourite animal, bird or pet? Here is an easy step-by-step approach by well-known artist Don Conroy. He shows you how to draw a great variety of subjects – trees, flowers, birds, and wild and domestic animals. So, whether you have never picked up a pencil before, or already have a keen interest in drawing, this book is for you!

This definitive book is a companion to the bestselling *Cartoon Fun* book.

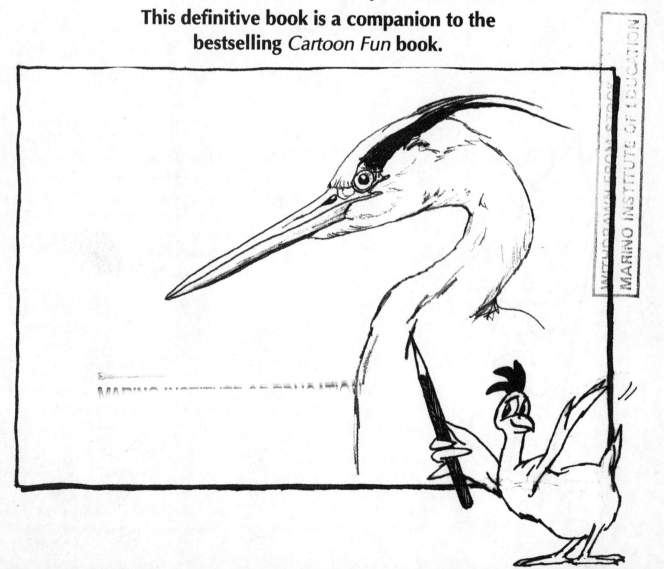

**Other books by Don Conroy
from The O'Brien Press**

First published 1994 by The O'Brien Press Ltd.,
20 Victoria Road, Rathgar, Dublin 6, Ireland.
Copyright © Don Conroy 1994
British Library Cataloguing-in-publication Data
Conroy, Don
Wildlife Fun
I. Title
823.914 [J]
ISBN 0-86278-385-2

The O'Brien Press receives assistance from
The Arts Council/An Chomhairle Ealaíon.
10 9 8 7 6 5 4 3 2 1

Editing, typesetting, layout: The O'Brien Press Ltd.
Cover illustration: Don Conroy
Cover design: The O'Brien Press Ltd.
Cover separations: Lithoset Ltd., Dublin
Printing: Guernsey Press, Channel Islands

WILDLIFE FUN

WITH

Don Conroy

The O'Brien Press
Dublin

To my family and friends

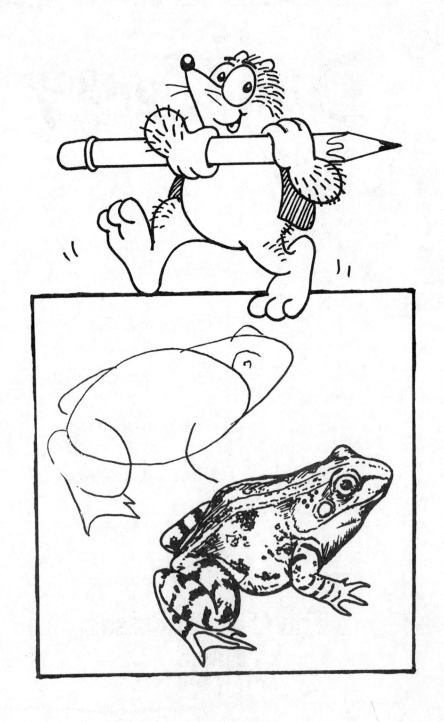

Contents

Introduction

HUMANS HAVE BEEN drawing animals for over thirty thousand years. There are exquisite examples in Stone Age cave paintings in Altamira in Northern Spain, and in other parts of the world. The human world and the animal world are deeply interwoven. This is lavishly depicted in paintings, weavings, carvings, symbols, poetry, song, myth and story. The natural world is full of mystery and beauty but it does not easily reveal its secrets to the undiscerning eye. Drawing can be a special way to discover its wonders. It can help us develop our skills of observation, besides giving us hours of pleasure.

The great poet William Blake challenged us all to 'see the world in a grain of sand, and heaven in a wild flower'.

I hope you enjoy this book, and that it will help kindle your creative fires.

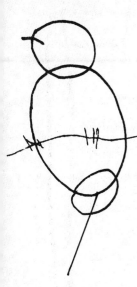

To study birds you need a sketch book and binoculars.

Try to draw or paint the bird near an object like a branch or leaf.

This is to show its size in proportion to its immediate environment.

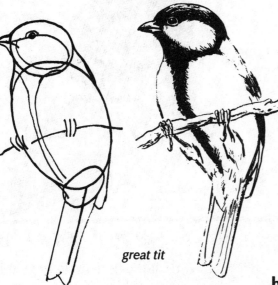

great tit

Watercolour pencils are wonderful for sketching birds.

When the colour is done, dip a small brush in water and brush it on your already coloured sketch, for some lovely watercolour effects.

The wren is our second smallest bird (the goldcrest being the smallest). As well-known as any of our birds, and often featured in songs and poems, it is reddish-brown in colour and heavily barred.
A wren's tail is often cocked up, giving the bird a perky look.

↑ A LITTLE PEN E WASH

DETAILED LINE AND BRUSH DRAWING OF A PAIR OF WRENS

The male and female are similar in appearance, and have surprisingly loud voices for such tiny birds. The wren feeds on insects. During the winter months wrens sometimes roost communally for added warmth, and a nest box suits them very nicely. Present all year round.

The rarest of our falcons. Merlins are found in remote parts of the country – boglands and mountain areas but will visit estuaries in wintertime. These sketches were done with a felt-tipped marker. It is important to try and get the stance and attitude of the bird correct.

Here are some pencil sketches of a mute swan. The bottom one is a dry-brush painting and line drawing. This beautiful bird is found on lakes, rivers and canals. The male is called a cob, and the female a pen. The young are called cygnets and are grey in colour until mature. Swans are present all the year round.

A rather comical-looking member of the auk family. In summer its plumage is black and its belly white, with orange legs, a pale grey face and a large multicoloured bill. In winter the bill sheds its coloured outer shell, and the puffin appears more auk-like, less clownish.

Found on grassy plateaux above sea cliffs, and on slopes on islands, it lives in a burrow which it digs out. One egg is laid in early May. A young puffin has brown downy feathers, and a small bill. The parents feed the young for about forty days, after which its plumage is developed and the young puffin must make its way to sea. Puffins spend the winter at sea.

MALLARD

SONG THRUSH

ROBIN

Drawing a young barn owl

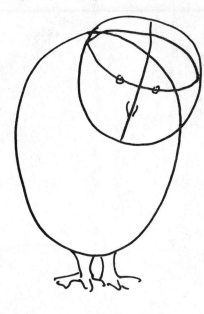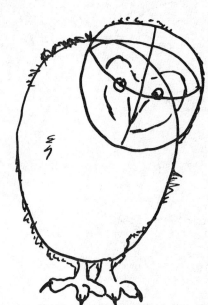

**As before, start off with the egg shapes,
remembering the stance and attitude. Broken lines suggest downy feathers.**

These are sketches of
young owlets which hatched
out in my own bird house
in the back garden.

BIT OF AN
UGLY DUCKLING
I KNOW,
BUT IT
WILL GROW
INTO
A BEAUTIFUL
OWL
LIKE
ME!

TRY THIS POSE!

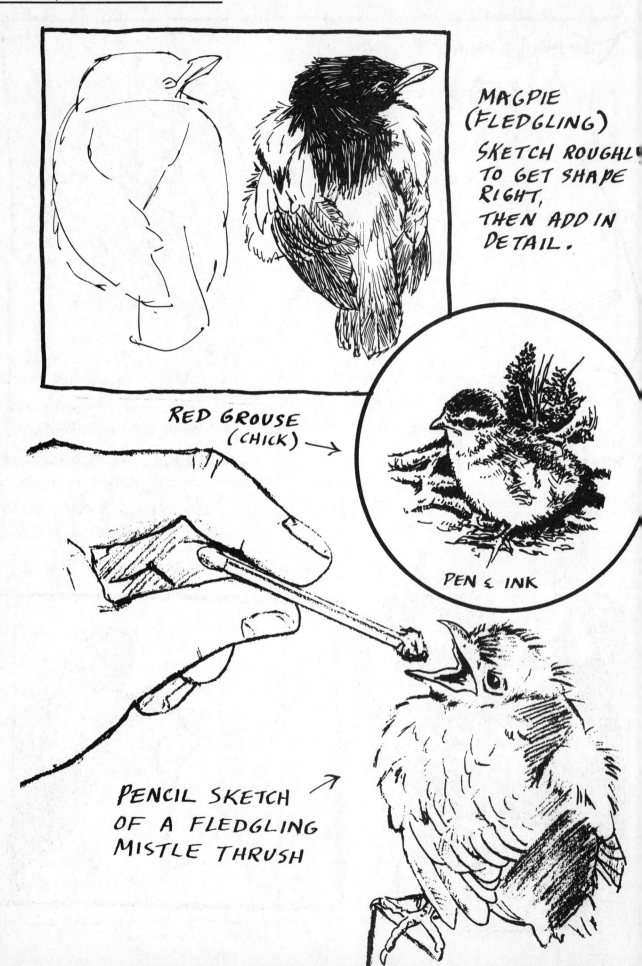

MAGPIE
(FLEDGLING)

SKETCH ROUGHLY
TO GET SHAPE
RIGHT,
THEN ADD IN
DETAIL.

RED GROUSE
(CHICK) →

PEN & INK

PENCIL SKETCH
OF A FLEDGLING
MISTLE THRUSH

Barn owls are quite scarce but present all year round.

Loose pencil sketch of a pair of barn owls

The ghostly hunters of the night, barn owls are mostly spotted in car headlights, passing over a country road. They tend to live close to human habitation, on farmland and on the outskirts of towns. They feed mainly on rats and mice. They fly silently, but their call is a long strangled shriek. They nest in old farm buildings or hollow trees, and will use nest boxes.

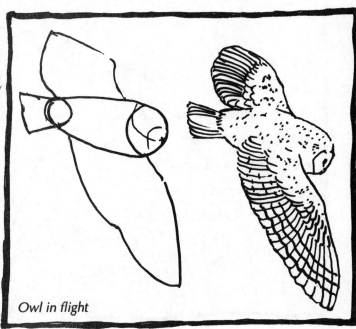

Owl in flight

KESTREL

Our commonest falcon.
Male has a grey-blue head and nape, and its back and
wings are reddish with dark spots. Female is larger,
and chestnut-coloured with black barrings.

DIPPER

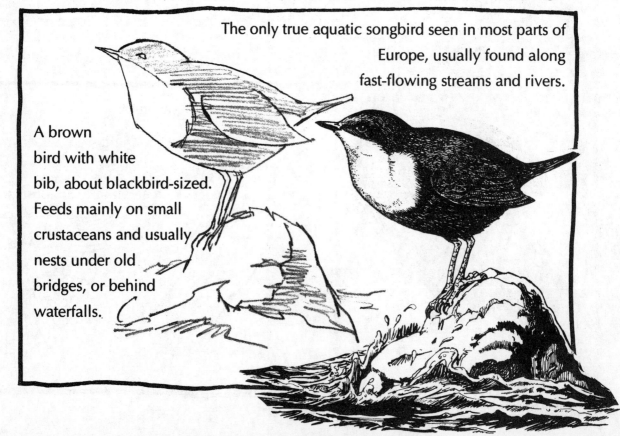

The only true aquatic songbird seen in most parts of
Europe, usually found along
fast-flowing streams and rivers.

A brown
bird with white
bib, about blackbird-sized.
Feeds mainly on small
crustaceans and usually
nests under old
bridges, or behind
waterfalls.

Here you see a quick sketch to get the pose right. Pen and ink detail on the right.

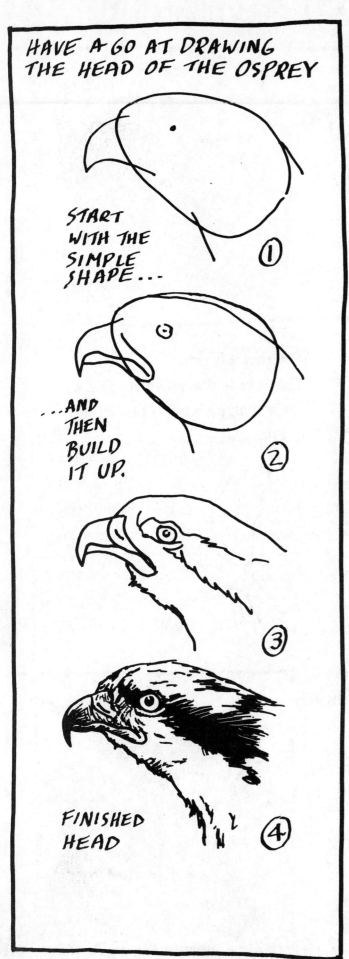

HAVE A GO AT DRAWING THE HEAD OF THE OSPREY

START WITH THE SIMPLE SHAPE...

①

...AND THEN BUILD IT UP.

②

③

FINISHED HEAD

④

These sketches were done in Loch Garten in Scotland. The osprey is a rare visitor to Britain and Ireland from Africa. It lives exclusively on fish. An osprey crashing into the water to catch a trout is a most spectacular sight. They may even catch two at a time.

In the USA artificial nests have been placed high up on poles in an effort to encourage this rare bird to breed.

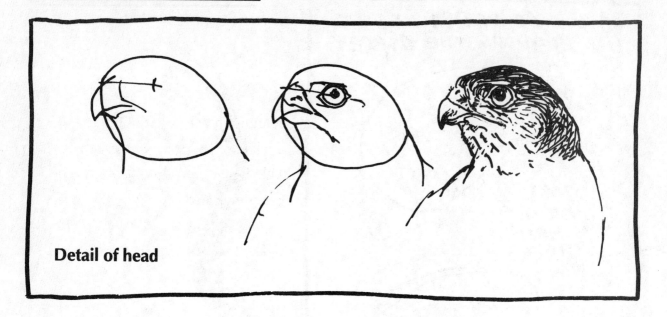

Detail of head

A common bird,
found in parks,
woods and farmland.
The female is larger
than the male.
During mating,
sparrowhawks put on
spectacular aerial displays.

Overhead flight.
This is how one normally gets to
see a sparrowhawk – flitting
overhead.

Detailed pen and ink
drawing of sparrowhawk
mantling its prey.

Example of
sparrowhawk's foot.

A majestic falcon found in wild and remote areas, the peregrine nests on cliff faces and mountain ledges. Its flight is swift and strong, and it is a slate-grey colour. Peregrines feed mainly on pigeons and sea birds, and have a shrill 'kek-kek-kek-kek' call. The female is larger than the male.

Peregrines move to estuaries to hunt in winter. A pair has successfully nested in Dublin City for several years.

Here is a detailed picture of some peregrines.

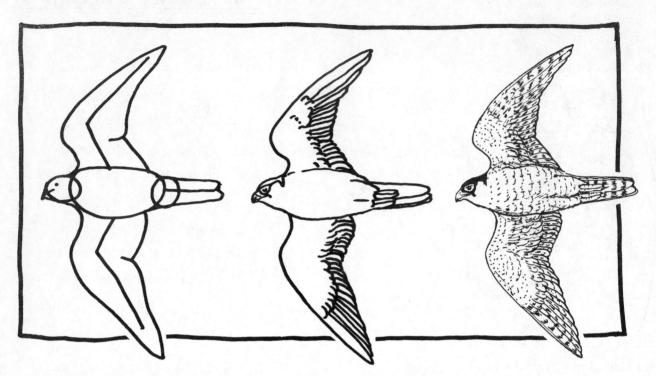

Start off with these simple egg shapes
and build up the drawing.
Leave detail until last.

Detail of juvenile
peregrines with
adult in flight.
Techniques included:
lightly sketching the bird
with pencil, then detail with
ballpoint pen and ink. Brush
strokes form black areas.
A blade was used
for highlights.

A tawny owl sitting on a branch. With pencil rough out shape of
head and body, and add heart-shaped face. When shape is correct
rub out unnecessary lines. Detailed drawing with felt-tipped marker.

Although common and widespread in Britain, the tawny
owl is completely absent from Ireland. Its call is used
frequently for night scenes in movies.

Owl on branch.
Brush, india ink and pencil technique.

STUDY OF TAWNY OWL HEAD
USING ALMOST DRY BRUSH
WITH INDIAN INK.
STROKES VERY LOOSE.

WE'RE QUITE FAMOUS REALLY.
EVEN SHAKESPEARE QUOTED US...
"TU-WHIT, TU-WHO - A MERRY NOTE,
WHILE GREASY JOAN DOTH KEEL THE POT."
                    -LOVE'S LABOUR'S LOST

**Brush on glossy board. The background was painted
solid black, then a blade was used to scrape white lines into it.**

SPARROWHAWK

Here's an example of how to use leaves along with a brush and paint. For this painting, I used real leaves, painted and pressed on paper, and then drew a sparrowhawk with a brush when the paint was dry.

The grey heron is alert and motionless in shallow water. Ever-watchful, it waits patiently for a fish or some small creature to come within range. Then it strikes with its dagger-sharp bill, stabbing the prey and swallowing it whole.

The heron is a large, long-legged and long-necked bird, with a white head and dark streaks on its neck. Its yellow bill turns a bright pink colour during the breeding season. Herons nest in colonies or 'heronries' in trees.

Four or five pale greenish-blue eggs are usually laid, in a nest built by the female. Herons are present all year round, and can be seen along the seashore and in estuaries.

Detailed pen and ink drawing using ballpoint pen.

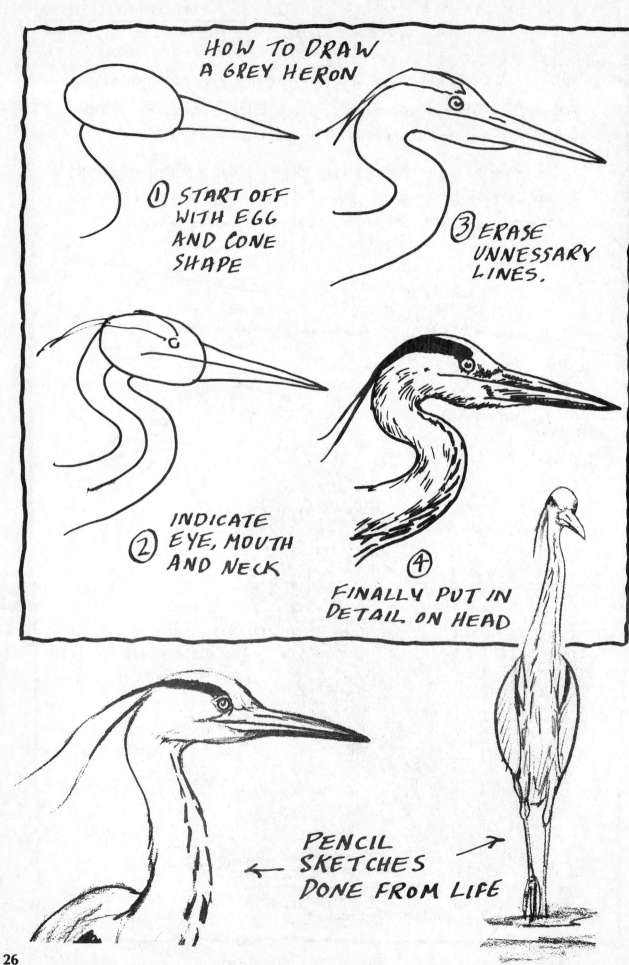

HOW TO DRAW
A GREY HERON

① START OFF
WITH EGG
AND CONE
SHAPE

② INDICATE
EYE, MOUTH
AND NECK

③ ERASE
UNNESSARY
LINES.

④ FINALLY PUT IN
DETAIL ON HEAD

PENCIL
SKETCHES
DONE FROM LIFE

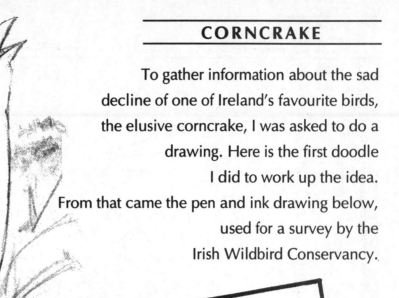

CORNCRAKE

To gather information about the sad
decline of one of Ireland's favourite birds,
the elusive corncrake, I was asked to do a
drawing. Here is the first doodle
I did to work up the idea.
From that came the pen and ink drawing below,
used for a survey by the
Irish Wildbird Conservancy.

SAVE THE CORNCRAKE

You can help by letting us know if
you hear corncrakes this year.
Please write giving the following

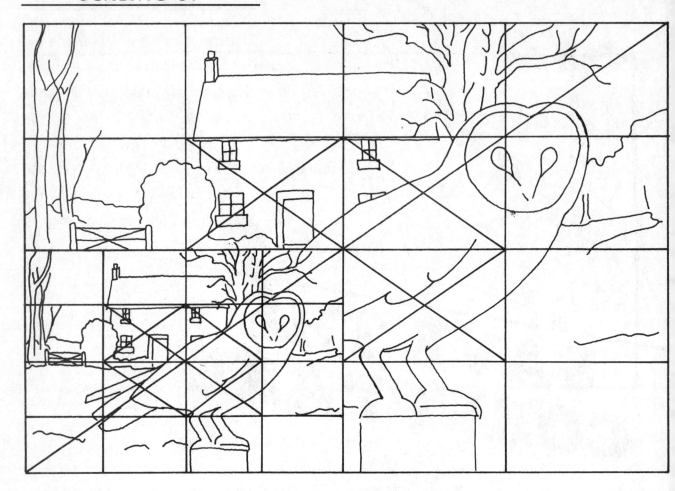

This technique can be used to scale up photographs or sketches. Make a grid and place it on top of your sketch, scale it up as shown above. Transfer the information using the grid lines as your guide.

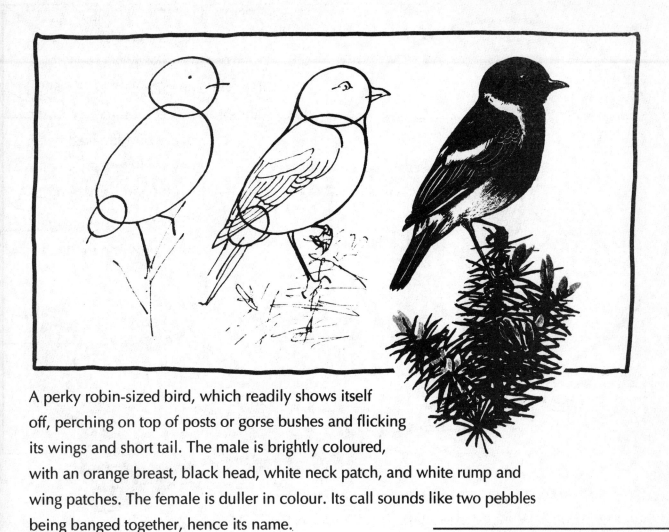

A perky robin-sized bird, which readily shows itself off, perching on top of posts or gorse bushes and flicking its wings and short tail. The male is brightly coloured, with an orange breast, black head, white neck patch, and white rump and wing patches. The female is duller in colour. Its call sounds like two pebbles being banged together, hence its name.

KINGFISHER

A shy, secretive bird found along slow-running rivers and streams. It is a dazzling blue and green colour with an orange-red underside. The kingfisher has a large head and a long beak, but short wings and tail. Male and female kingfishers look similar.

HEN HARRIER

The sight of the hen harrier gliding low over a bog is a very special treat. The male is a pale grey colour, with a white underbelly. The female is larger, and brown in colour, with a brown and white streaked belly. They have yellow legs, a white rump, and a barred tail.

Hen harriers feed on small birds and mammals.

HERE IS A NOT-TOO-DETAILED DRAWING OF A HEN HARRIER FLYING OVER FIELD, SKETCHED WITH FELT-TIPPED MARKER

RARE VISITOR TO IRELAND

VERY DETAILED MARSH HARRIER

3B PENCIL SKETCH OF MONTAGU'S HARRIER

FIELD SKETCH (SPAIN '89.

RN OWL
NADEA CO. KILDARE '85
2M EVENING

BARN
OWL POST
HOPPING'
AT EDGE OF FIELD

DON
CONROY

QUATERING

BAEN OWL
HUNTING
OUER FIELD

* CALL
A LONG
STRANGLED
SHRIEK

OWL
FINALLY
CAUGHT RAT
AFTER AN HOUR
SEARCH

TRANSFERRED
RAT FROM
FEET TO
BILL

LARGE
HEAD

PATTERN
ON BARN OWL'S
PLUMAGE

EYES
BLACK

HEART
SHAPE
FACIAL
DISC

GOLDEN
BUFF
COLOUR

WHITE
UNDER-
PARTS

How to draw a badger

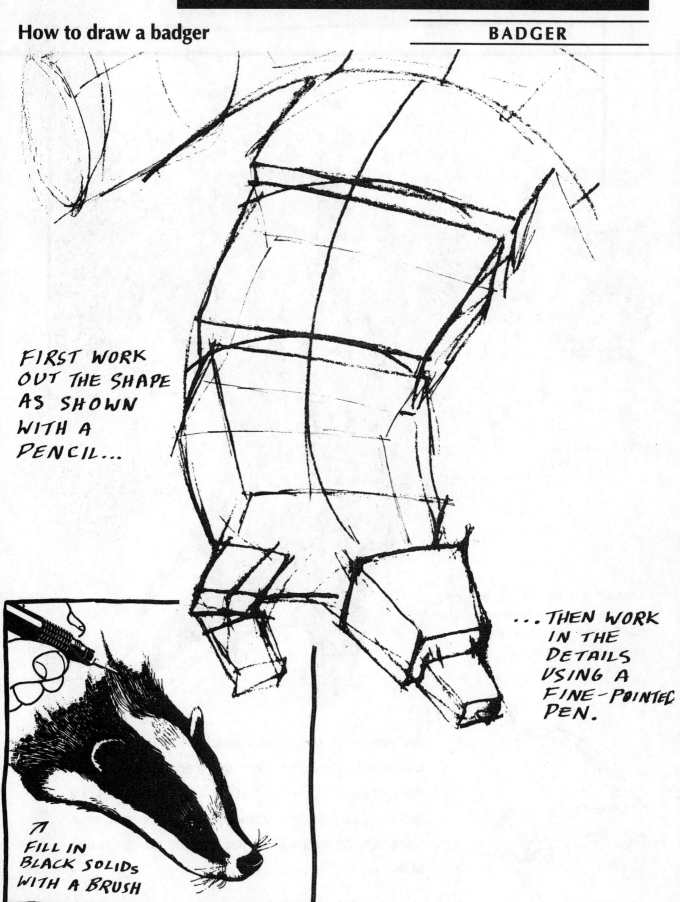

FIRST WORK OUT THE SHAPE AS SHOWN WITH A PENCIL...

...THEN WORK IN THE DETAILS USING A FINE-POINTED PEN.

↗ FILL IN BLACK SOLIDS WITH A BRUSH

Detailed drawing of badger emerging from a sett. A small brush was used to black in the sett and the stripes down its face and legs.

Badgers are widespread throughout Ireland. Mainly nocturnal, they are shy and wary animals, and therefore seldom seen. The male is larger than the female. Badgers breed annually, and a litter of three is common. Young badgers may be seen above ground from May to August at dawn.

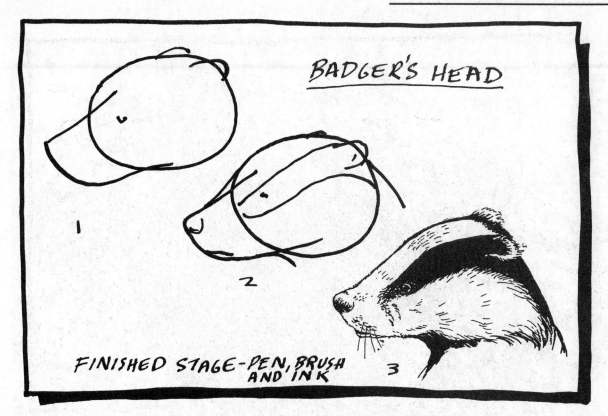

BADGER'S HEAD

FINISHED STAGE-PEN, BRUSH AND INK

1

2

3

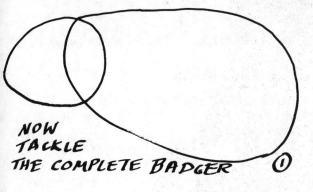

NOW TACKLE THE COMPLETE BADGER ①

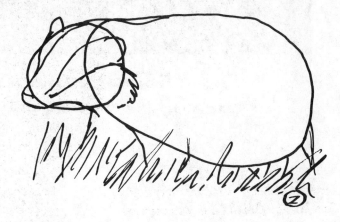

②

A badger's home, which is below ground, is called a sett. It is a series of connecting tunnels and chambers, and may house two or more badger families. Badgers are omnivorous – they will eat earthworms, mice, rats, young rabbits, blackberries, acorns and beech nuts, among other things. Their sight is poor and they rely mainly on hearing and sense of smell to locate food.

COMPLETE PEN & INK

This badger was first sketched with a pencil,
then pen and ink. A brush and a blade were used to get different effects.

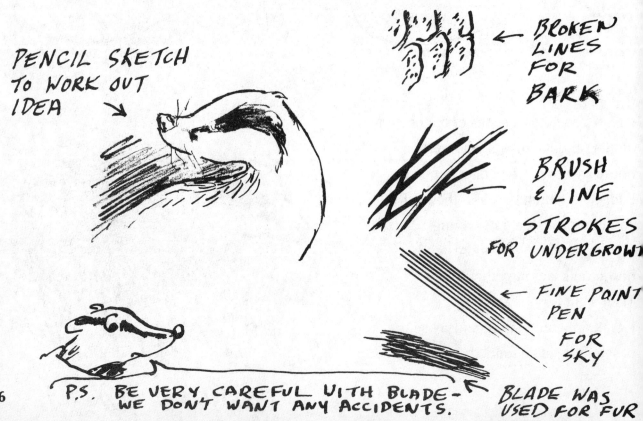

PENCIL SKETCH
TO WORK OUT
IDEA →

BROKEN
LINES
FOR
BARK

BRUSH
& LINE
STROKES
FOR UNDERGROWTH

← FINE POINT
PEN

FOR
SKY

P.S. BE VERY CAREFUL WITH BLADE -
WE DON'T WANT ANY ACCIDENTS.

BLADE WAS
USED FOR FUR

*Study of the head of
an otter emerging from
water, using watercolour pencil.*

The otter is a member of the Mustelidae family, as are the stoat, badger and pine marten. It is a carnivore, and is widespread in Ireland along river systems and coastal areas. Its nesting place is called a 'holt', a large burrow in the bank of a river or stream.

Shy and mainly nocturnal, the otter has a long slender body, a flat head, a tapering tail and webbed feet. Young may be born at any time of the year, two or three per litter. Otters eat a variety of foods: eels, fish, crabs, crayfish and aquatic insects.

THIS LOOKS EASY TO DRAW ... I THINK

The red deer, the largest of the three species of deer found in Ireland. Native to Ireland they are found mainly in Donegal, Wicklow and Kerry.

Their coat is reddish-brown, with a cream-coloured rump. In winter the coat gets darker and the hair longer.

A stag has multi-pointed antlers which he sheds every April. A new pair begins to grow immediately. A royal stag is one with a twelve-pointed antler.

Make a rough sketch to get the stance correct. Add detail but keep the drawing loose.

OH WELL, PRACTICE MAKES PERFECT.
OH DEAR! I MADE A MESS.

HEDGEHOG

Originally found only in deciduous woodlands, hedgehogs are now seen almost everywhere in Ireland. They are often seen in hedgerows, copses, meadows and suburban gardens. They are active mainly at night. The male is called a boar, the female a sow, and the young are called piglets, because of their pig-like appearance. Beetles, caterpillars and earthworms make up most of the hedgehog's diet, but it will also eat birds' eggs, slugs and snails.

Hedgehogs hibernate in winter and are ready to breed in April. Three to five young are usually born in early summer. They begin to sprout bristly spines, which are modified hairs raised in defence, within hours of birth. The young grow over two thousand spines, compared to the adults' five thousand or so.

Originally from America, the grey squirrel was introduced to Britain and Ireland around the beginning of the twentieth century – first to Britain, and then to Ireland from England in 1913.

It prefers to feed on the ground, and now lives in many areas formerly occupied by the red squirrel. With its chestnut flanks, yellowish-brown head and grey-brown body it is often confused with the red squirrel.

FANCY DRAWING MY COUSIN? HAVE A GO, AND DON'T WORRY ABOUT MAKING MISTAKES. MICHELANGELO MADE A FEW AS WELL YOU KNOW. P.S. I DON'T MEAN A TURTLE.

Usually sandy to brown in colour, although black rabbits are common in certain areas. White underside to tail. Rabbits feed mainly on grasses, but will also eat cereal crops, roots, and young trees.

Rabbits were first brought to Ireland in the twelfth century by the Normans. They breed between January and June, and up to eight rabbits are born a month after mating. Rabbits can breed in their first year.

Sitting position and running. Note broken lines to indicate fur.

HOLD STILL PLEASE

Common throughout Ireland, and has adapted successfully to urban life. Reddish-brown fur. Bellies, lower part of their faces and tips of their tails are white, eyes are an amber colour.

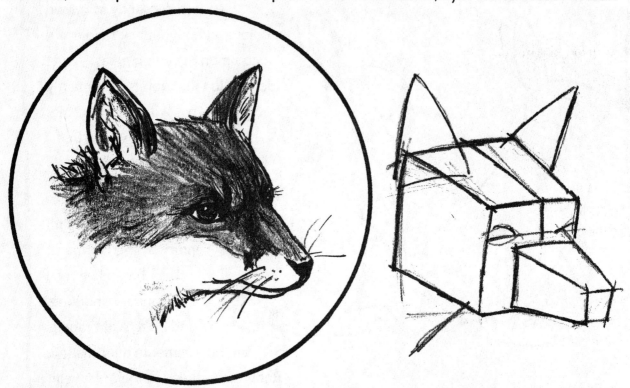

Build up the head of a fox. Start off with pencil. Use the box shapes and when you're satisfied with the shape of the head ...

... rub out unnecessary lines and add details. Brush and pencil.

SEPT 9th '89 CASTLE TOWN WOODS
WARM/DRY   NEAR LAKE (CELBRIDGE)

FOX CAME FROM WOODS
MOVED ALONG DIRT TRACK

FOX APPEARED AS SOON
AS THINGS BECAME QUIET

LATER
FOX
SAT AT EDGE
OF FIELD
FOR SEVERAL MINUTES

(ALWAYS WARY)

GREY SEAL

Common all around the Irish coastline, though they prefer breeding sites
facing the Atlantic Ocean. Their coat is very variable, from black
to mid-grey, with the male (bull) darker than the female (cow).

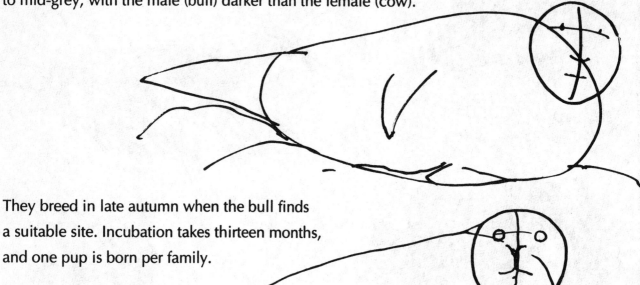

They breed in late autumn when the bull finds
a suitable site. Incubation takes thirteen months,
and one pup is born per family.

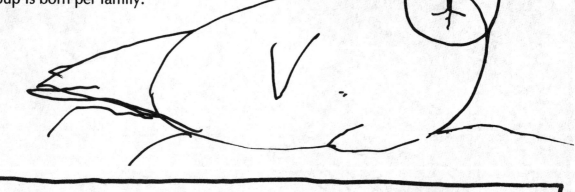

Grey seals feed on fish, crabs and lobsters. Their
heads are more pointed than a common
seal's, which is more rounded.

Finished drawing – grey seal lying on rocks

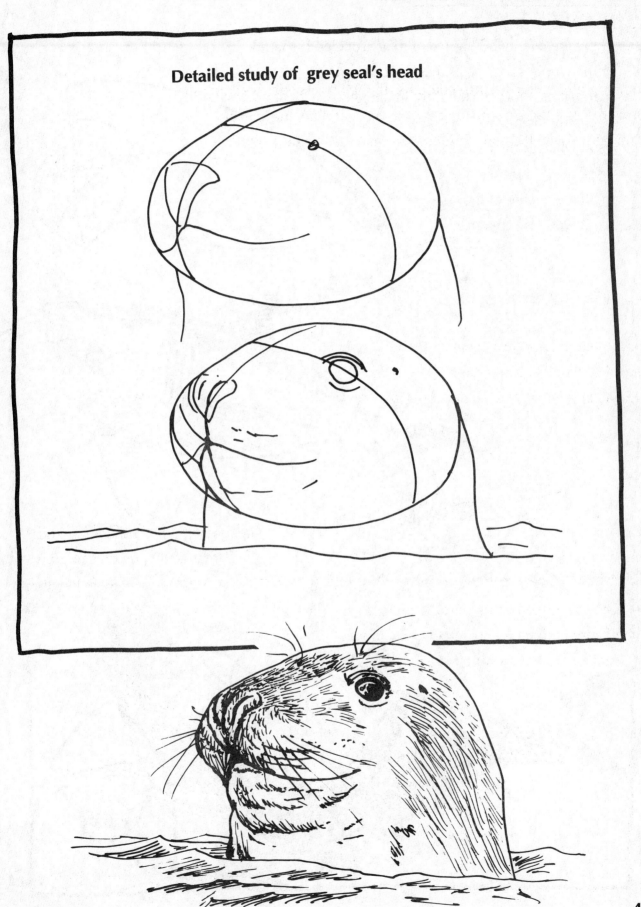

Detailed study of grey seal's head

There are over two hundred and fifty species of shark in the world, and nine of these are known man-eaters. Probably the most infamous one, after the movie 'Jaws', is the great white shark. Ferocious yet fascinating, this huge fish is found in all the oceans of the world yet it is very rare.

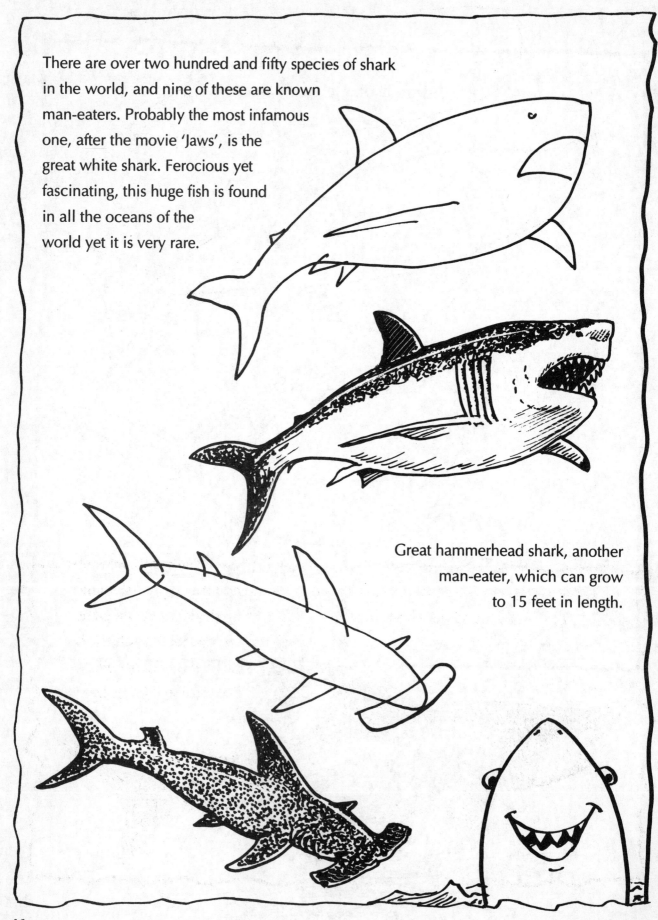

Great hammerhead shark, another man-eater, which can grow to 15 feet in length.

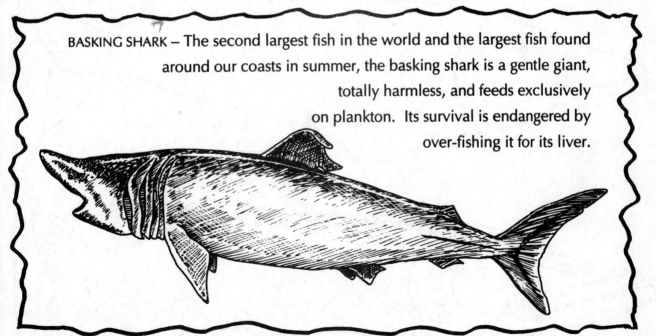

BASKING SHARK – The second largest fish in the world and the largest fish found around our coasts in summer, the basking shark is a gentle giant, totally harmless, and feeds exclusively on plankton. Its survival is endangered by over-fishing it for its liver.

STICKLEBACK

Gets its name from the sharp spines on its back. Kingfishers and other predators must swallow it head first or else the spines will stick in their throats. Sticklebacks live in ponds, streams and rivers.

PIKE

Lives in lakes and slow-moving rivers where there is plenty of cover. There he'll wait in the water weed to ambush a passing fish. Pikes can catch all sorts of aquatic creatures, from fish, frogs and rats to young ducks. Some pike have lived up to 33 years, usually females.

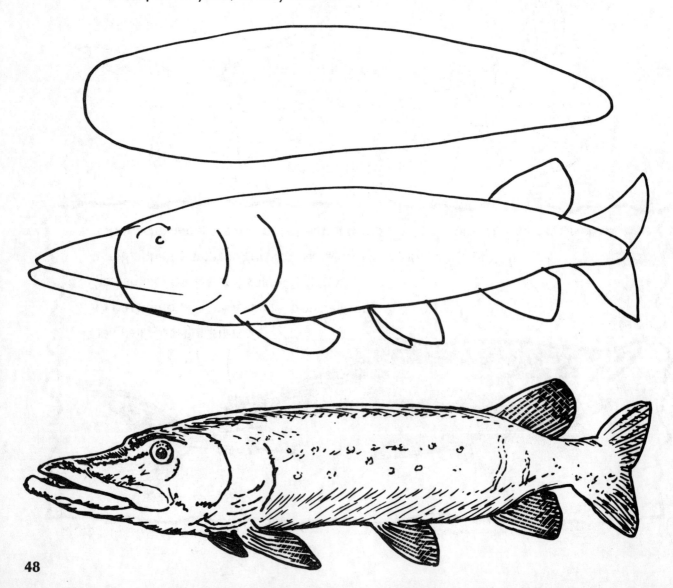

Often seen around the Irish coast. Gets its name from the resemblance of its beak to an old-fashioned gin bottle.

Flipper, flukes and upper body are slate-grey in colour.

Adult bottle-nosed dolphins may grow to twelve feet long.

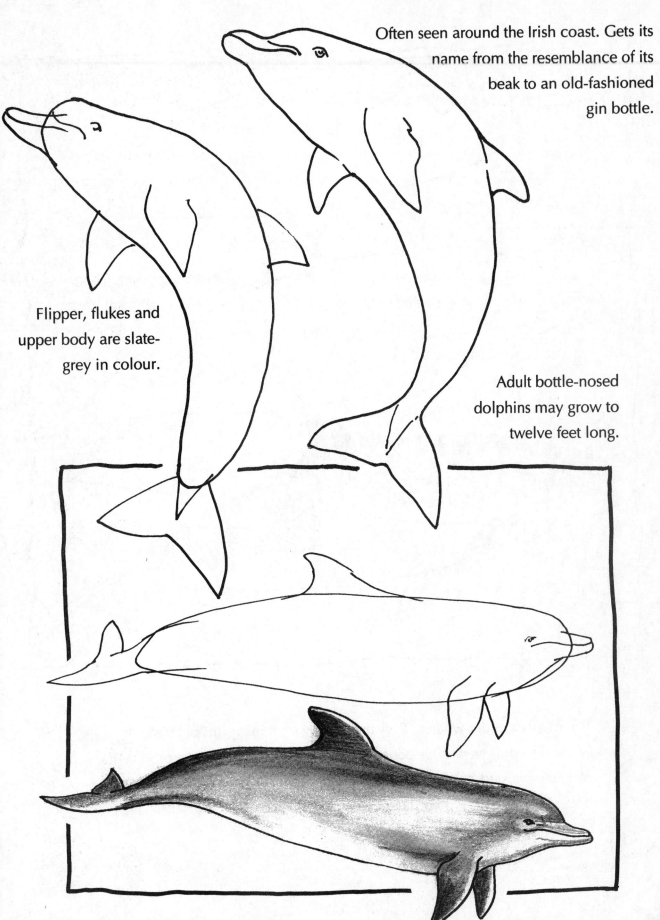

The smallest of our whales. They are usually seen in groups of three, although when migrating very large schools have been recorded. The porpoise has a distinctive round head and short triangular dorsal fin at the mid-point of its back. It can be up to two metres long, and feeds mainly on sand eels, crabs and mackerel.

Once widely distributed in European waters, the humpback whale is now rare, due to over-hunting by commercial whalers at the beginning of the century. It grows to about sixteen metres in length. It has a small dorsal fin two-thirds of the way down its back, and two large wing-like flippers. Its head is covered in bumps.

AT THE ZOO

HERE ARE A NUMBER OF SKETCHES DONE WITH A 3B PENCIL, OF ANIMALS AT THE ZOO. I TRY TO LOOK FOR THE CHARACTER OF THE ANIMAL AND ITS FORM.

IT DOES NOT MATTER HOW ROUGH THE SKETCHES ARE. DRAWING FROM LIFE WILL HELP YOU BUILD UP CONFIDENCE, AND HELP YOU OBSERVE MORE.

THE ZOO IS A WONDERFUL PLACE TO BRING YOUR SKETCHBOOK AND PENCIL TO.

THESE SKETCHES WERE DONE WITH PEN & INK

TAKE YOUR TIME WHEN DRAWING. THE MAIN THING IS TO ENJOY YOURSELF.

I first sketched the head
of the cheetah with a
felt-tipped marker, then I
roughly sketched in the two
cheetahs sitting together,
but I still tried to keep
the drawing loose and fresh.

Quick outline of chimpanzee swinging. Put in detail later with a dip pen.

Quick pencil sketch of chimpanzee's face. Put in loose detail with a 3B pencil.

55

How to construct the head of an African elephant

Quick outline with pencil to suggest movement of elephant, then worked on later, putting in small details with felt-tipped marker.

DON'T
FORGET
2B PENCILS
ARE GREAT
FOR DRAWING
WITH

Follow the simple shapes, build up the crocodile and erase unnecessary lines. Put in a little loose detail.

REMEMBER LEAVE DETAIL UNTIL LAST

Quick action sketch of
heads of lion and lionesses

Later on do
more detailed
drawing with
dip pen from original sketch.

**Roughed-in shape. Do a
more detailed study
using a 3B pencil.**

SCRAPER BOARD

A scraperboard can give wonderful results. Here is a drawing of one of my favourite birds, a barn owl. Since owls are mainly seen at night, the white on the black can be most effective. Sketch what you want. To transfer it on to the scraperboard, go over your sketch with a ballpoint pen to make an impression on the board. Then take your scraper and remove the black areas you don't want.

RED SQUIRREL

This is like sketching in reverse. Scraperboards and the tools that go with are available in art shops. Use an ordinary blade if you don't have a scraper.

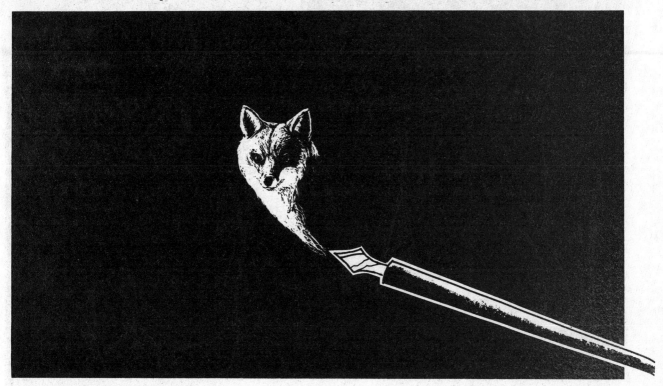

For children I would suggest using crayons, say a yellow one first.

Spread it over paper, then cover the yellow crayon with a black crayon. Scrape away a design using a coin.

Draw a swallow on some cardboard, then carefully cut around the swallow. Now you have two stencils.

1.

2.

Lay the cardboard stencil (1) on paper and sponge in colour. Let it dry, then move it along and sponge on a different colour.

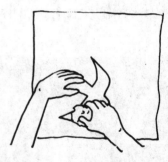

For a different effect, sponge around the sides of the cut out swallow (2) with a colour. Repeat process with different colours.

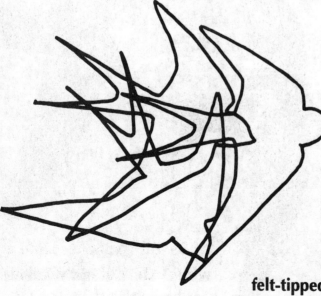

Another effect can be got if you draw around the swallow form (2) with different coloured felt-tipped pens to make interesting patterns.

MOBILE 1

Materials: pliers, wire coathanger, card, scissors, adhesive tape.

To draw swallow shape
simply follow guide shown
on paper, then reverse paper
and with a
soft pencil (2B) go over swallow shape.
Place paper on another piece of
card with swallow the right way
round and go over the
outline with a ballpoint pen.
This will transfer swallow onto
other pieces of card and can be
repeated many times.
Then cut out the swallows.

Bend a coathanger into a
wire circle. Cut out swallow
shapes and fix them onto
wire with adhesive tape.

BIRDS OF PREY

Draw bird shapes on black paper.

Cut out eagles, hawks and
vultures and place on
window with blue tack.
This can be a very
effective way to dress
your bedroom window.

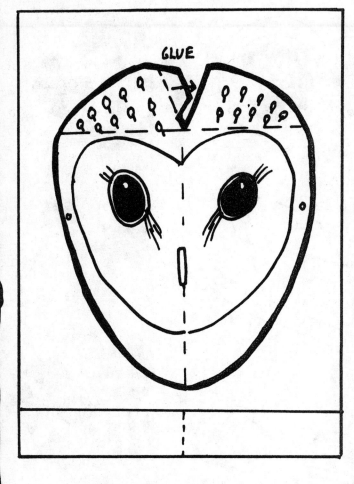

GLUE

Make an owl mask:

1. Get a firm piece of cardboard. Draw owl face on it.

2. Cut slot to take beak. Punch two holes for eyes (ask for help from a grown-up if you are using a scissors or needles to make the holes, we don't want any accidents).

3. Fold long piece of card for beak as shown on diagram. Round off to make it like a beak. Glue it from the back.

4. Cut an elastic band and make two holes at side of mask and tie on the band.

5. Colour the mask if you wish with markers or poster paints.

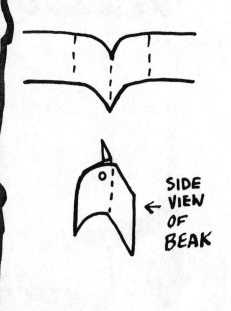

SIDE VIEW OF BEAK

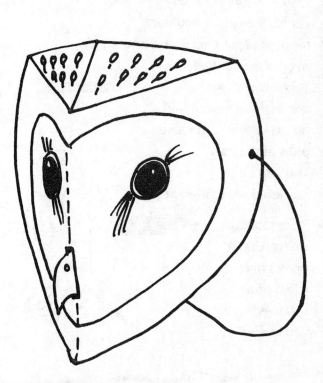

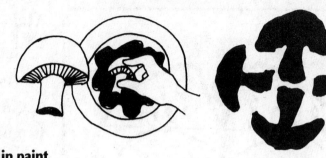

- Cut a mushroom in half, dip it in some paint, then print on paper to make different patterns.

- Slice a carrot, cut stars in different sizes, again dip it in paint and print.

- Cut a potato in half, then cut different patterns, dip into paint and print.

- Put holes all the way around a potato with a pencil. Then stick a pencil in either side, to make a roller. Dip it in some paint and roll pattern on the paper. Move it in different directions to produce interesting patterns.

- Leaves make great prints. Paint the leaf, lay it on paper, then place another piece of paper over it and smooth it over with your hand. Take away paper and leaf and you should be left with an attractive print of the leaf. This can be reprinted with different leaves.

- Remember the sparrowhawk drawn over a leaf print I showed you earlier!

Draw a fish on cardboard, then cut it out.

Glue the fish onto a piece of wood, then dip it into paint. Lay a newspaper on the table, then get your white paper and start to print your fish by putting pressure on the wood.

The newspaper will catch any excess paint.

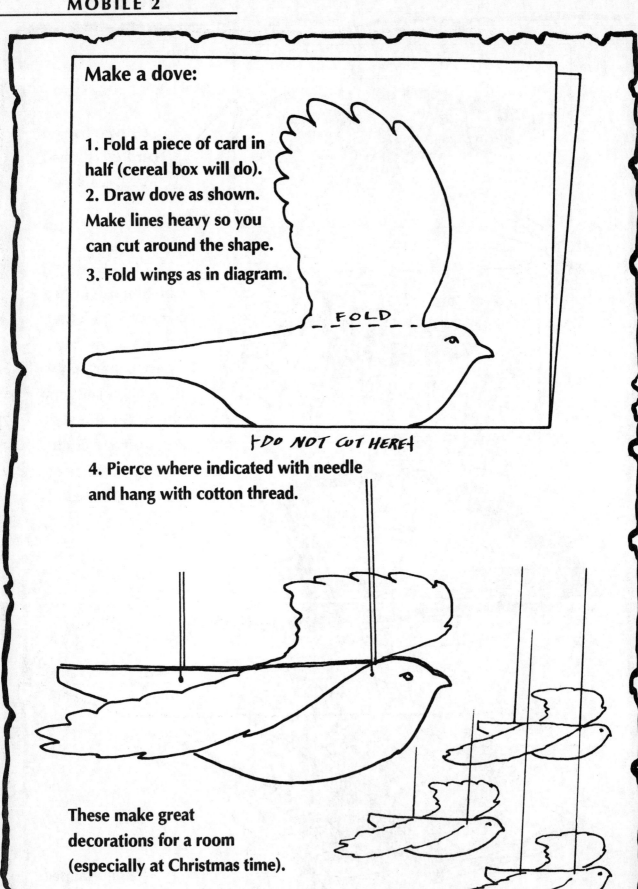

Make a dove:

1. Fold a piece of card in half (cereal box will do).
2. Draw dove as shown. Make lines heavy so you can cut around the shape.
3. Fold wings as in diagram.

FOLD

┼DO NOT CUT HERE┼

4. Pierce where indicated with needle and hang with cotton thread.

These make great decorations for a room (especially at Christmas time).

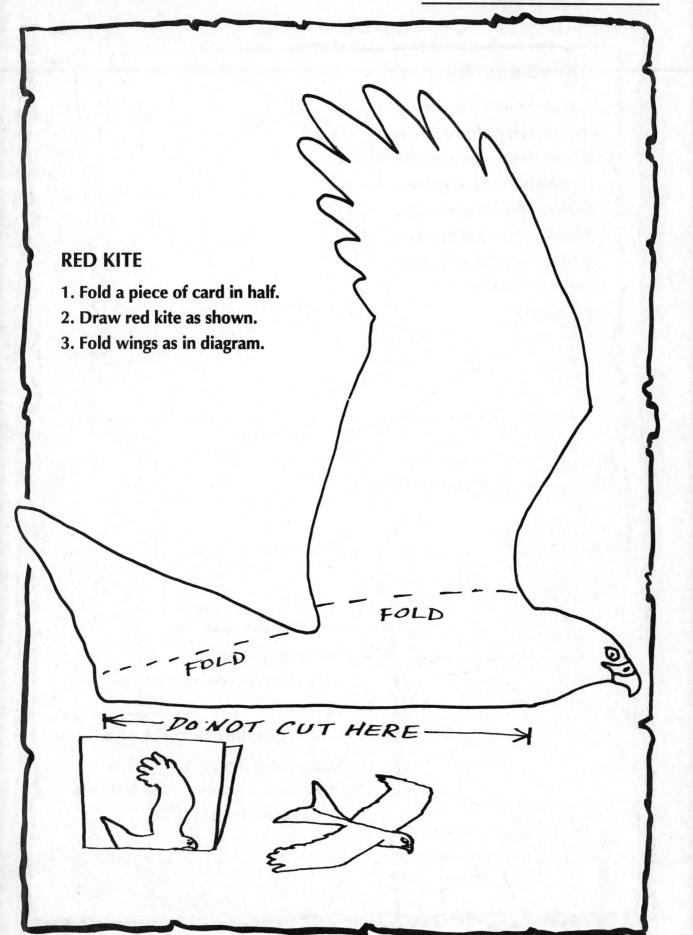

RED KITE

1. **Fold a piece of card in half.**
2. **Draw red kite as shown.**
3. **Fold wings as in diagram.**

FOLD

FOLD

DO NOT CUT HERE

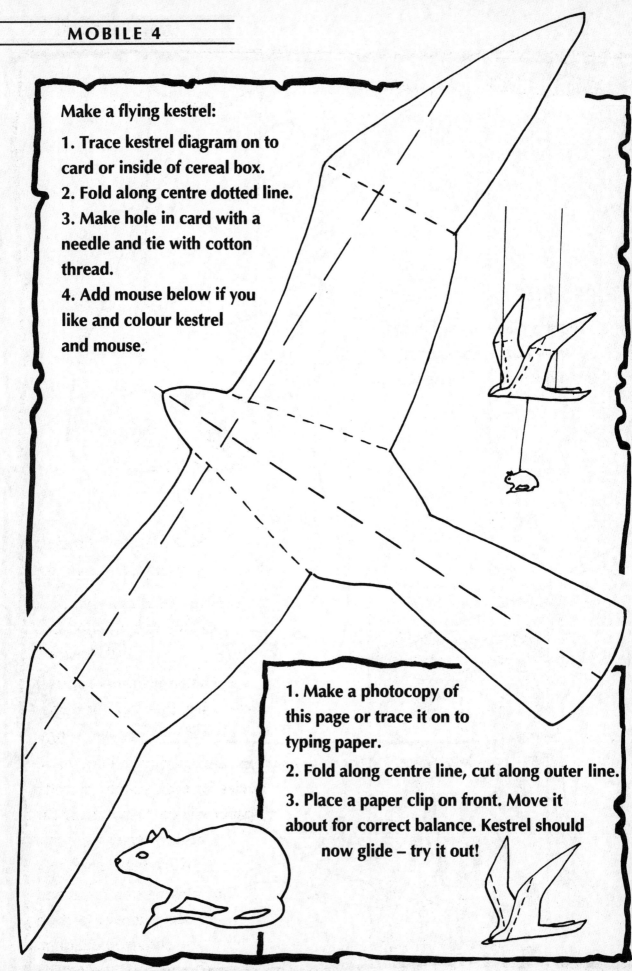

Make a flying kestrel:

1. Trace kestrel diagram on to card or inside of cereal box.
2. Fold along centre dotted line.
3. Make hole in card with a needle and tie with cotton thread.
4. Add mouse below if you like and colour kestrel and mouse.

1. Make a photocopy of this page or trace it on to typing paper.
2. Fold along centre line, cut along outer line.
3. Place a paper clip on front. Move it about for correct balance. Kestrel should now glide – try it out!

Make an owl model:

1. Take two toilet rolls.

2. Squeeze one at one end, then cut along the dotted line with scissors.

3. Flatten the other roll and draw wing, then cut out shape. This will give you two wings.

4. Get a penny and draw two circles for eyes, yellow or white paper will do. Leave shape for beak. Then draw in eye with a felt-tipped pen.

5. Glue on wings and eyes and decorate with pattern shown in diagram.

Look for the overall form in an object.
Here are some examples.

PETS & FARM ANIMALS

Animals can be very difficult to draw, as they are nearly always on the move. Nevertheless, it is very rewarding and challenging to study them. Persevere and you will develop speed and skill.

Your pet if you have one is an ideal subject, or you can walk in the park to observe ducks. Carry a notebook when you can, and a 3B pencil or watercolour pencils.

1 2 3

ABOVE: A CAT. THE LINES SUGGEST ALERTNESS

1. START WITH CIRCLE

A kitten in four stages

2. ADD EARS, EYES & MOUTH

3 PUT IN DETAIL AND RUB OUT UNWANTED LINES

4 FINISHED SKETCH.

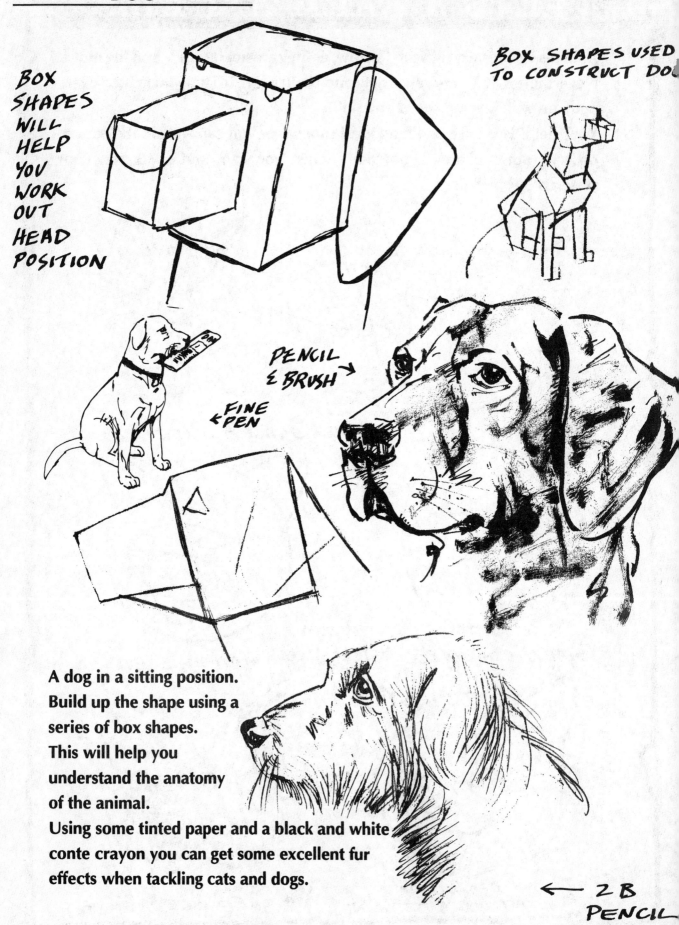

BOX SHAPES WILL HELP YOU WORK OUT HEAD POSITION

BOX SHAPES USED TO CONSTRUCT DOG

PENCIL & BRUSH →

FINE ← PEN

A dog in a sitting position. Build up the shape using a series of box shapes. This will help you understand the anatomy of the animal. Using some tinted paper and a black and white conte crayon you can get some excellent fur effects when tackling cats and dogs.

← 2B PENCIL

HOW TO DRAW A FARM PIG

① ②

ACTION SKETCH OF PIG

①

②

DRAW A GOAT

①

②

QUICK FIELD SKETCH OF SHEEP

Try to tackle this horse's head by building up shapes as shown.

The sketch below was made watching horses in a field towards evening.

Building up a horse's head in three easy stages.

The muscles of a horse are easily observed.
The box shape is to give you the overall body shape.

How to show movement with loose pen strokes.

↳ *THE HOOF OF A HORSE*

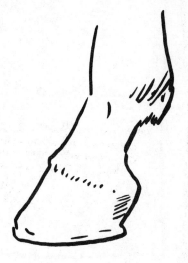

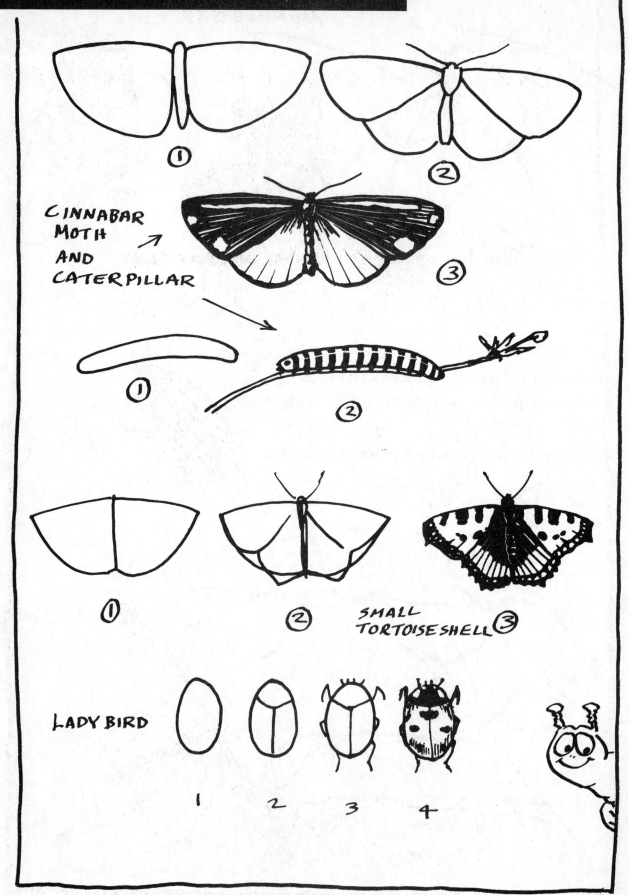

CINNABAR MOTH AND CATERPILLAR

① ② ③

① ②

① ② SMALL TORTOISESHELL ③

LADY BIRD

1 2 3 4

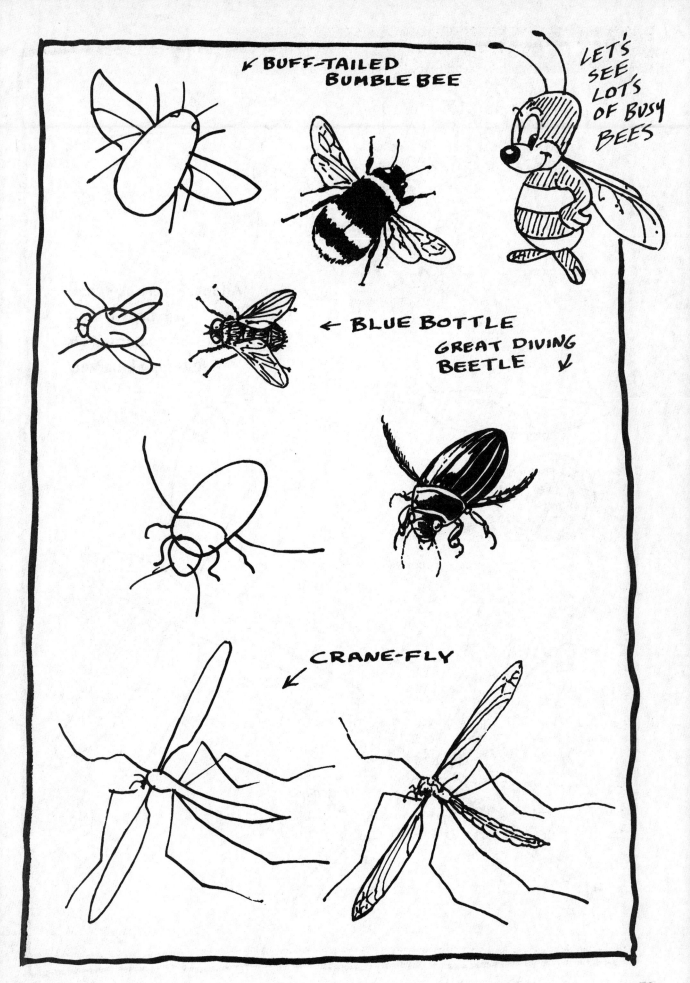

← BUFF-TAILED
BUMBLE-BEE

LET'S
SEE
LOTS
OF BUSY
BEES

← BLUE BOTTLE

GREAT DIVING
BEETLE ↓

CRANE-FLY

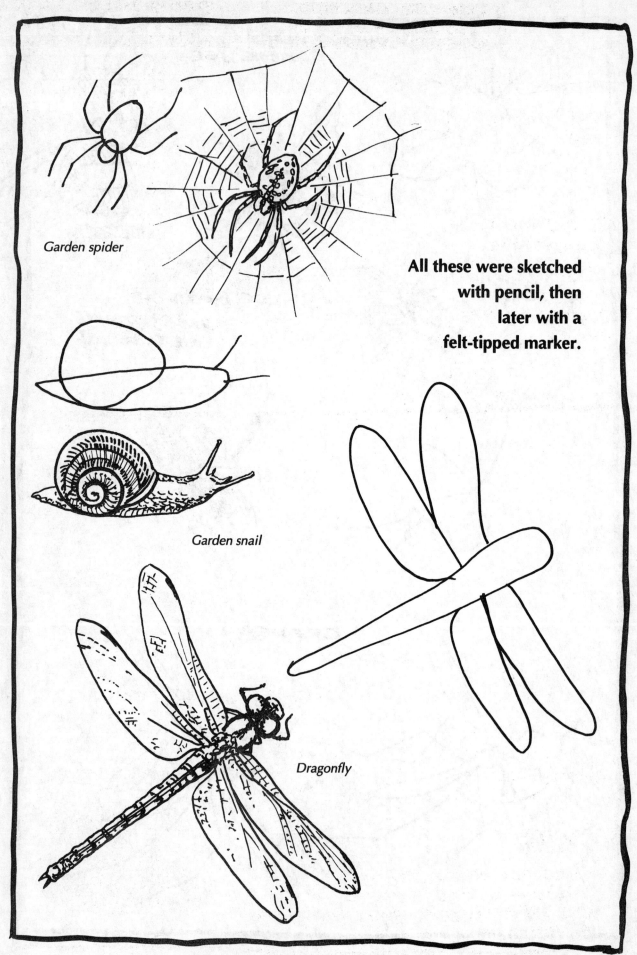

Garden spider

All these were sketched with pencil, then later with a felt-tipped marker.

Garden snail

Dragonfly

SNAKES

USING A SIMPLE
EGG SHAPE AND
CURVED LINE
YOU CAN GET
REQUIRED SHAPE
OF SNAKE

BOA CONSTRICTOR
(PYTHONS AND THE
ANACONDA)
ARE THE LONGEST
SNAKES IN THE
WORLD

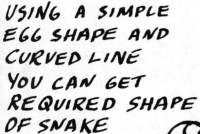

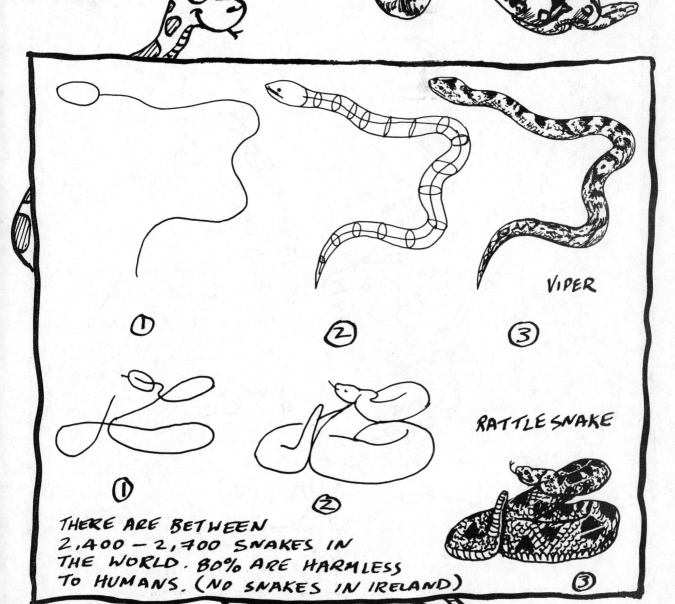

VIPER

① ② ③

RATTLESNAKE

① ②

THERE ARE BETWEEN
2,400 – 2,700 SNAKES IN
THE WORLD. 80% ARE HARMLESS
TO HUMANS. (NO SNAKES IN IRELAND)

③

Frogs are excellent swimmers and never stray far from water although they can jump well on land. They feed mainly on insects and slugs. Life span is up to six years. Frog eggs hatch after two weeks, the tadpoles developing into froglets in late summer.

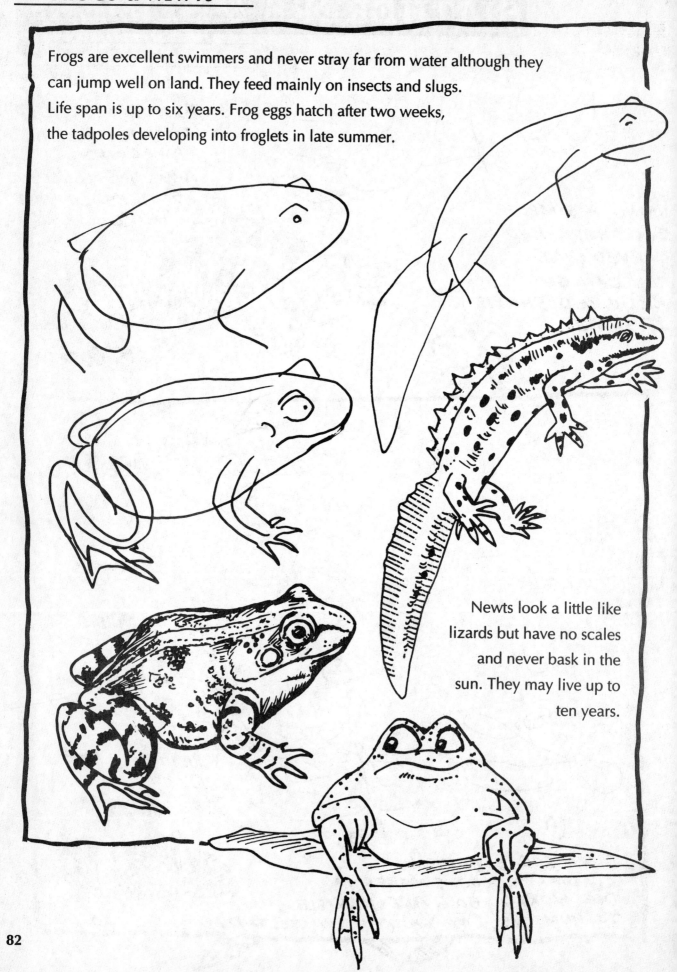

Newts look a little like lizards but have no scales and never bask in the sun. They may live up to ten years.

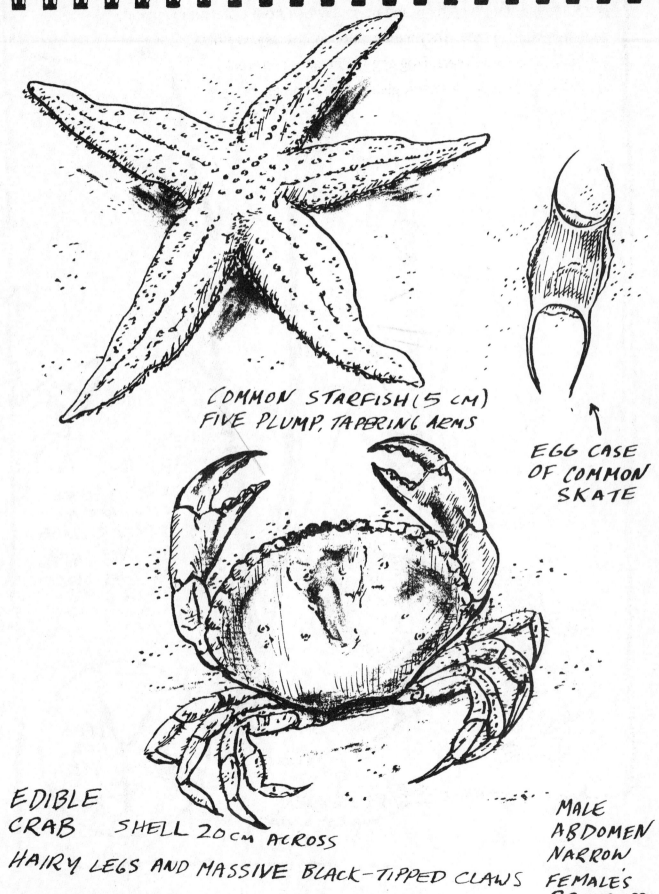

COMMON STARFISH (5 CM)
FIVE PLUMP, TAPERING ARMS

EGG CASE
OF COMMON
SKATE

EDIBLE
CRAB   SHELL 20 CM ACROSS
HAIRY LEGS AND MASSIVE BLACK-TIPPED CLAWS

MALE
ABDOMEN
NARROW
FEMALE'S
BROAD 83

TREES IN WINTER

THE SECRET OF DRAWING IS LOOKING FOR STRUCTURE OR FORM IN WHAT YOU DRAW.

MOST TREES ARE BASED ON A 'Y' SHAPE.

THIS IS VERY OBVIOUS IN WINTER TIME AS THE SKETCH ON THIS PAGE SHOWS

LOOK FOR THE 'Y' SHAPE

IT WAS DRAWN OUTDOORS USING A 3B PENCIL

Dead tree stumps can
be very attractive
to draw. Start with the
outline using a 3B pencil, then add detail.

An old rustic post

Here is a detailed drawing of a hollow tree. Hard lines were drawn with a
H pencil, then a 3B pencil was used for soft shading.
The owl is almost overlooked even though he is clearly drawn.
This was the effect I was trying to achieve.

Flowers and plants can be
difficult subjects, but have a go.
These were drawn with a
felt-tipped pen.

A pencil might be easier to begin
with. Later if you can manage with
a colour pencil, the effects are
lovely. Always look for the form or
shape. Detail should always
be left until later.

PRIMROSES

BRACKEN

YELLOW FLAG
(IRIS)

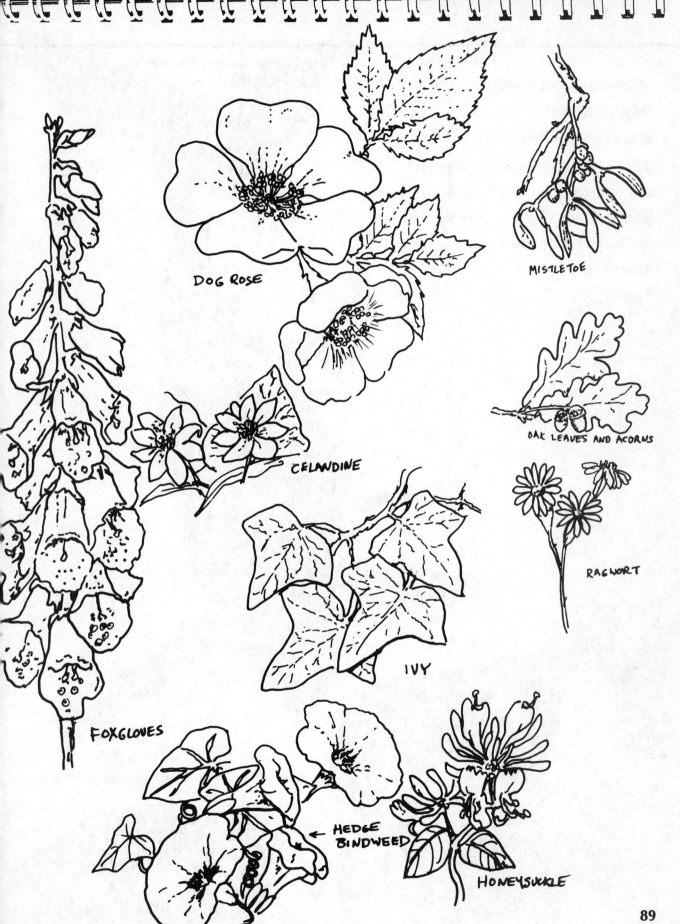

DOG ROSE

MISTLETOE

CELANDINE

OAK LEAVES AND ACORNS

RAGWORT

IVY

FOXGLOVES

← HEDGE
BINDWEED

HONEYSUCKLE

Silhouettes can make lovely pictures. Here are a few examples:

1. Humpback whale with her young.
2. Horse in a field.
3. Fox going home after a successful night's hunting.

1.

2.

3.

Tree using indian ink and two different sizes of brush, a large one to cover big areas, and a small one for the branches.

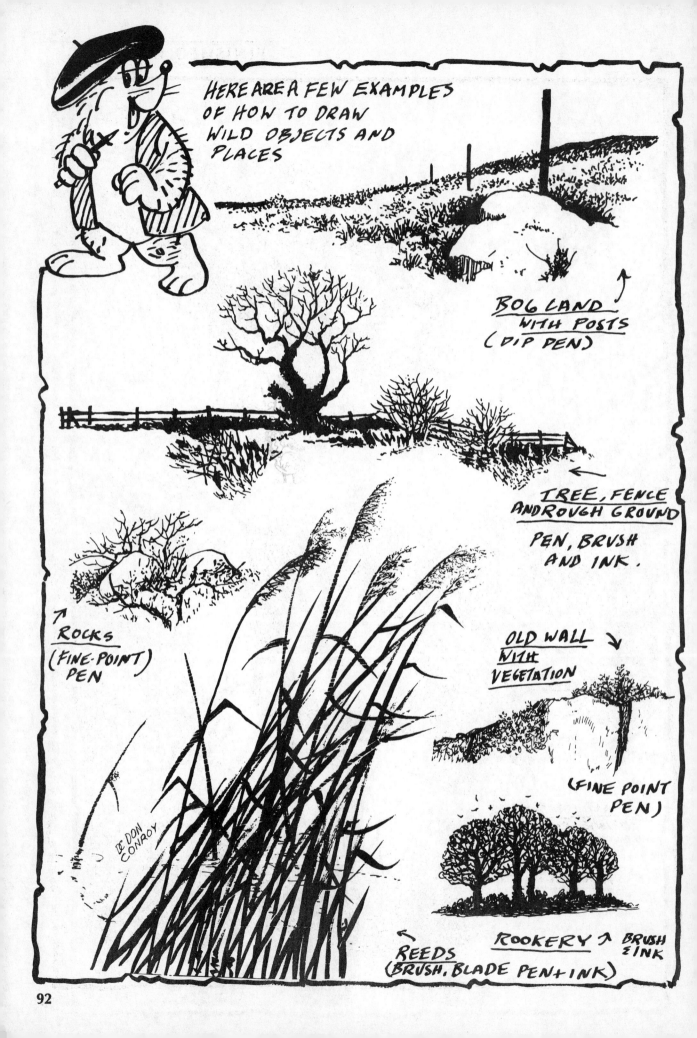

HERE ARE A FEW EXAMPLES
OF HOW TO DRAW
WILD OBJECTS AND
PLACES

BOG LAND
WITH POSTS
(DIP PEN)

TREE, FENCE
AND ROUGH GROUND

PEN, BRUSH
AND INK.

ROCKS
(FINE·POINT)
PEN

OLD WALL
WITH
VEGETATION

(FINE POINT
PEN)

REEDS
(BRUSH, BLADE PEN + INK)

ROOKERY BRUSH
& INK

© DON
CONROY

OLD STUMP →
(FINE POINT
PEN.
BRUSH + INK)

HOLLOW TREE
(FINE POINT PEN)

FIRE IN GORSE
(FINE POINT PEN)
BRUSH + INK

HEATHER →
(DIP PEN)

FINISHED DRAWINGS

FOX
(FINE-
POINTED
PEN)

BADGER
(FINE-POINTED
PEN + BRUSH)

PHEASANT
IN FLIGHT
(DIP-PEN)

RAT
(FINE-POINTED PEN)

ROOK
ON BRANCHES
(BRUSH
+ FINE
POINTED PEN)

BARN OWL
IN FLIGHT

BRUSH,
BLADE &
FINE-POINTED PEN

94

RED FOX
(FINE POINT PEN)

RED GROUSE
(FINE POINT PEN)

BADGER
(PEN, BRUSH + INK)

(DIP PEN)

KESTREL
HOVERING

IRISH HARE
(FINE PEN)

HAVE FUN!

BARRED
OWLS
(PEN, BRUSH
AND INK)

FAST-FINDER